I0446570

Praise for *Maverick Soul.*

"Guido and Michael lay it down with their real stories from how they crashed through that million-dollar ceiling. They share contrarian lessons on how they have hustled their way to financial independence and built a life on their own terms. If you're daydreaming about ditching the 9-to-5 and doing your own thing, you've got to give this one a read."

—Scott Fluhrer, VP Marketing, PMWeb

"If you're looking for real business advice on trusting your gut, putting your knowledge into action, and designing your own path to success, you've got to check out this book. It's like a treasure chest of smart moves for your entrepreneurial journey."

—David Butterwolf, Venture Capital Works

"Every digital creator is following the same gurus and doing the same things. Everyone is reading the same "How to get followers" handbook and over time most people end up doing the same thing. If you're looking for an edge, a secret sauce for getting ahead of the pack, give this book a read."

—Martin Lindson, Former VP Digital, Wadd Communications

"Maverick Soul makes us rethink various points of view, shows us how to see opportunities where others see problems, to question the trends of gurus, to think critically about various current situations, such as the impact of the growth of AI, and what difference this will generate in the inequality we have today. Furthermore, it presents a very particular perspective on growth, development, and the importance of being truly present!"

—Fabio Sausen, Founder and CEO, Fabio Sausen
Productivity Booster!

GUIDO PICUS AND MICHAEL VICTOR LANCE

MAVERICK SOUL

Unlocking Personal and Business Wealth: Contrarian
Wisdom & Growth Hacks for Monetizing Your Ideas -
Real-Life Stories of Marketing Mavericks

Book cover design by Michael Victor Lance

ISBN: 9798870413129

Imprint: Independently published

Some of the images in the book were designed with AI-assisted technologies.

What is a Maverick?

"Mavericks are <u>visionaries</u> who want to achieve what's never been achieved before. They're not fans of the status quo and will shake things up. Mavericks tend to be innovative, influential, daring, and direct—with a remarkably high tolerance for taking chances. They believe there is a bigger, better, stronger, faster way."

What is a Soul?

"The soul is the spiritual or immaterial part of a human being or animal, regarded as <u>immortal.</u>"

Maverick Soul:

An immortal visionary

This book is inspired by Michael Lance, my brother from another mother and dedicated to the three most important people in my life: Marel, Freyja and Kristjana.

CONTENTS

FOREWORD BY DAVID BUTTERWOLF

Ever feel like you're spinning in circles with your entrepreneurial dreams? Drowning in an ocean of YouTube tutorials, Instagram reels, and an ever-growing stack of e-books and online courses, yet finding real progress just out of reach? *Maverick Soul* is your lighthouse in these choppy waters.

Guido and Michael don't just talk the talk; they've walked the path you're on, faced the same challenges, and emerged victorious. In these pages, they share their two-decade-long journey, packed with contrarian lessons and wealth-building secrets that have the power to transform your entrepreneurial dreams into reality. They cut through the noise, helping you forge a prosperity mindset, create a killer marketing strategy, write content that resonates, and turn your digital business into a money-generating machine.

Maverick Soul is not just a guide; it's a wake-up call to stop consuming and start creating. It's about making those audacious dreams a reality. If you're ready to break free from the content consumption loop and step into the role of a true maverick, this book is your first step. Welcome to the journey of a lifetime.

INTRODUCTION: HOW I BROKE FREE

My journey has been a wild one. Picture this: a restless soul, kind of like Picasso, always itching to shake things up. That was me, bouncing around 8 different countries, crossing paths with everyone under the sun—from bankers, hippies, PhD's, spies, shamans, Harvard MBAs, prime ministers, kitesurfers, startup founders to millionaires. I've hustled and flipped my first bike at 13, worked as a financial analyst in banking in South America, started one of the most innovative bar concepts in Ecuador, and even sold ecommerce software for Amazon.com across Europe. I also founded a successful digital marketing agency, which was acquired by Deloitte. I'd do it all over again if given the opportunity.

"If you're worried about the cost of getting started...you should see the price of staying exactly where you are."

Be your own muse.

I've also been in your shoes. There was a time when I binged on 100's of YouTube videos until my eyes ached, hoarded newsletters, and stockpiled ebooks and courses on crushing it as an entrepreneur. I was stuck in a content coma, downloading more than I was doing. I was glued to an ever revolving wheel of content downloads, not progressing fast enough on my goals.

From our first breath, society tries to box us into roles, teaching us to admire and follow those corporations and gurus above us. But within each of us is a spark, a chance to rise, to see beyond these invisible chains. Unless kindled early, this spark often fades, distracting us from our calling. Our world is brimming with so-called "gurus" trying to show us the way, often leading us astray. This dependency on them, masked as guidance, is a dangerous loop we find ourselves in. This methodology, under the guise of leadership, perpetuates an addictive cycle where the individual is continually drawn to these guru figures. It's like they've all read the same "How to get followers" handbook. It's reminiscent of the Stockholm Syndrome, where one's identity becomes so intertwined with your captor. In the quest for self-improvement, there's another trap—the "StuckHome Syndrome," a term coined by my co-author Michael Victor Lance. It's about being so dazzled by the guide that you miss the guidance. Rather than focusing on the content of guidance, you are often entranced by the figure delivering it. Instead of absorbing the lesson, you get hung up on the person teaching it. This not only hampers your personal development but also fuels the cycle of dependence on such pseudo authority figures. But remember this: True growth comes when we listen to the message and take control of our journey. If you start acting on the knowledge you gain and trust yourself more, you can outgrow the need for any guru. Be your own guru, that's the key. Embrace your knowledge, take that step, believe in your own genius, and let the world see the guru within you.

I'm not some miracle-gro guru. I'm just a guy who broke free and built several successful ventures. This book is for you—the newbie, the startup founder, the solo pioneer, the 9-to-5er dreaming of more, and the career-switcher. I'm about to drop 21 raw, real-deal stories, contrarian tips, and mental hacks from my global business escapades. Just as Dale Carnegie's book *How to Win Friends and Influence People* is written about psychology but used as a guide to better conversations, this book uses my 25 years of experience in business and startups as a metaphor for the best business practices for success. There is no traditional chapter outline, you can start anywhere in the book. Each story is based on true events, my experience, and packed with lessons I learned in the trenches. As you explore the stories, you'll discover actionable insights to help you trust yourself more, apply what you've learned, and carve out your path to unstoppable business success. Let's turn your knowledge into action and most importantly into revenue!

"Promoting yourself can be an uncomfortable proposition but let me put you at ease. This is not about you. It's about offering your gifts to the world."

A MAGICAL NEW WORLD

This is the most amazing time to be in business. Imagine: A billion (1,000,000,000) people will need training and new skills by 2030. Artificial intelligence is giving us uberhuman creative thinking powers. You will be able to grow two-person businesses to $1+ million in revenue with smart automation tools. Isn't this just the most thrilling time to pursue your ambitions? If we had been born in any other era and in other countries, this connection we have right now wouldn't even be possible. Had I been born at any other time in history I couldn't have been writing this book. It's kind of magic; you can design any product and within seconds it's available to the entire globe. You can create a video and people from the US to Australia might be watching, learning and being inspired by your words. Write a blog and someone in the UK might be pondering your insights over their morning tea. Imagine getting a call to speak at a conference halfway across the world because of something you wrote or imagined. It's real and it's happening now.

1 Year = 365 Opportunities!

The 2020s will bring a storm of technological disruption, ready to alter our entrepreneurial landscape. Artificial intelligence (AI) alone is poised to massively improve human decision-making, and businesses that leverage AI will thrive. The 2020s are shaping up to be a rollercoaster of change, especially in the entrepreneur space. AI is already nudging its way into our workflows, helping us make sharper decisions, and changing not only how we work but also how we think and create.

This decade will redefine the entrepreneurial model, enabling the successful operation of a $1 million enterprise with a lean team comprising just two pivotal roles: the flow orchestrator and the product maestro. The remaining functions could be efficiently managed through strategic outsourcing to AI and skilled freelancers. We're stepping into an era where being an independent inventor, a creative spirit, or a maverick soul is the norm. It's going to be a time of stark contrasts, with some people clinging to the old pre-AI ways of doing things while others leap into the new. This period will mark a divergence in operational approaches, with a clear demarcation between traditionalists and innovators. The truth is that we're going to have an extremely polarized society.

The entrepreneurial wave that's rolling in isn't just any wave—it's colossal. It's the kind of trend that reshapes landscapes. Some will ride it like pros, others will get tossed around a bit. But here's the thing: You're one of the savvy ones and by diving into this book, you're not just watching the wave—you're grabbing a surfboard and joining the ride.

Remember, this decade will not just be about making money but also about making a difference. As we navigate the 2020s, let's focus on building businesses that aren't just profitable, but also spray a little goodness in the world. Let's set sail into this new era, creating, shaking things up, and soaking in every bit of this incredible journey. Here's to the mavericks, the creators, and the wave riders—let's make this decade ours.

MASSIVE CHANGE AHEAD

Picture this: Born in the paradise of Aruba, ten years soaking up British culture, six years tasting the American dream, four years embracing the Ecuadorian lifestyle, a dash of time in Germany, a few spins around the Netherlands, and now catching the chilly yet stunning views of Iceland. That's my journey in a nutshell. And along the way, I've caught glimpses of the internet being born, waved goodbye to a job during the dotcom crash in 2009, and watched ecommerce and marketplaces grow like wildfires.

As I pondered on upcoming trends, something hit me. Have you ever thought about clouds and dirt? I'm not just throwing around buzzwords, I'm referring to the stark reality of the digital cloud versus the gritty, physical dirt under our feet. Take New York, for instance. It is a city of stark contrasts, where the high-flying tech elite cruise through their cloud-based empires while others hustle through the daily grind, all sharing the same sidewalks but living lightyears apart.

We entrepreneurs, we're the jugglers, balancing our cloud ventures with our feet firmly rooted in reality. We're the ones designing our own digital businesses, serving customers worldwide with a tap on our screens, chasing the dream of seamless transactions and recurring revenue. Meanwhile, those not aware of the digital realm are getting their hands dirty in the physical world, perhaps driving Ubers or flipping burgers, confined by the limits of their location.

This gap between the "cloud folks" and the "dirt folks" is only widening, and fast. Throw AI into the mix, and it's turbocharging this division. It's a catalyst either shooting some skyward or weighing others down, fostering a chasm between the voracious consumers and the prolific creators. This digital split isn't just about technology; it's creating a chasm in wealth and experiences. It's like a marathon where some are sprinting ahead, fueled by tech so advanced it seems like they're in an entirely different race.

AI is both the wedge and the lever and for many, it'll be a stumbling block, making life tougher. But for a select few, it'll be a turbo boost. AI is either going to make you a hyper-consumer, lost in endless scrolls on your phone, or a hyper-creator, harnessing it to build cutting-edge businesses that thrive and expand. As AI reshapes the landscape, we're seeing two societies drifting further apart.

As we navigate this mesmerizing digital wave, let's not just be passengers; let's also be pioneers. Let's not only create but also ignite creativity in others. And as we do, let's savor this incredible journey, where every click could bridge worlds, fostering a tad more equality in our increasingly digital society.

What do you say? Ready to ride the wave and perhaps create a few of your own?

THE STORY OF TWO SHOE SALESMEN IN ECUADOR

"A shoe company sent two salesmen to Ecuador to determine the market potential for their cowboy boot products. One salesman was sent to the Ecuadorian jungle, while the other salesman went to the mountain region. Both salesmen completed a basic survey of the target market and called back to the office. The salesman sent to the jungle reported: "None of the jungle natives here wear any shoes; there is no market for us here." The other salesman sent a message: "No one here wears any shoes; there is a huge market for us, send inventory fast!"

Back in the '90s, I was living in Ecuador and with some work buddies, we decided to launch a bar. The night before we opened, we brought in a shaman—yes, a real shaman—to bless the place. This guy was the real deal, chanting in Quechua, the language of the Inca Gods, and spitting fire from a concoction of alcohol and herbs. His words, "Manaraq Wiñachkaspa Allin Kawsay" meant "prosperity before growth." Wild! But here's the best thing—that bar turned into a goldmine. I still remember my business partner, Freddy, walking in the kitchen with large trash bags full of dollar bills spilling out.

"Manaraq Wiñachkaspa Allin Kawsay!"

You see, if you want to make it as an entrepreneur it's critical you think prosperity first, growth second. Your mind needs to be open to spot new opportunities, just like the shoe salesman did. To make it big, you've got to put prosperity before growth. It's like being on the lookout for opportunities with a mindset that's wide open.

Understanding the dance between prosperity and growth can change your life. They're like the dynamic duo of our brains, but they aren't quite the same. Think of it like planting a seed. You've got this tiny little thing that can grow into a massive tree. That's your growth – it's all about potential. But if you stick that seed on a rock and hope for the best, you're going to be waiting a long time. The seed needs good soil, and that's where prosperity comes in. It's the belief that the universe's got enough to go around for all of us.

So, why is it a big deal to get your prosperity game on point before diving into growing your business? Because it's like setting the stage, ensuring you're not just spotting opportunities but that you're also bringing wealth to yourself, which will enable you to do a world of good for other people as well. A prosperity mindset is a powerful energy that exists inside you that, once you choose to unleash, can open up a world of possibilities, beef up your bank account, and transform your life. But how do you cultivate a prosperity mindset? Two ways: 1) Ideas for the Masses and 2) Beware of Mitch the Analysis Monkey.

IDEAS FOR THE MASSES

You know how in school, some kids would hide their answers during tests? How we're often told to guard our brilliance? The fear whispers, "Shield it, or it will be stolen." It's funny how that doesn't change much when we grow up. At work, many think, "Keep that idea safe! Someone might steal it." But here's the twist: if you're always holding back, you might end up running out of steam. It's like always eating from your stored old food and never shopping for fresh stuff. But when you share your time and what you know, you're pushed to think more, to keep fresh ideas coming. By sharing, you light a fire within, pushing yourself to consistently innovate and evolve. And let's be real, those brilliant ideas you have? They're not just yours. Ideas are everywhere; you've just tuned in at the right time in the universe. Be the giver, and watch as the world opens up its treasures to you.

BEWARE OF MITCH THE ANALYSIS MONKEY

I'm guilty of overanalyzing the shit out of ideas myself. My first job as a financial analyst or analysis monkey at a bank involved squeezing the juice out of balance sheets and profit and loss statements. I'd spent days looking at the numbers and sleeping under my desk so I could continue analyzing ratios the next day.

"Don't be Like Mitch, The Analysis Monkey"

Entrepreneurs, especially solopreneurs, often find themselves at the crossroads of decision-making. But what happens when overthinking cripples you? Enter the shadowy realm of "analysis paralysis," a state where overanalyzing or overthinking prevents decisive action, causing stagnation, i.e., the StuckHome Syndrome. Imagine holding a treasure map, but instead of following it, you're busy debating the quality of the paper or the ink's shade. While pondering these details has its place, it can't overshadow the primary goal: *finding the treasure.*

Here's the crux: delays can cost you opportunities. Each moment you spend in overanalysis can be a moment where an opportunity slips away, a competitor moves ahead, or you get drawn back into the ever revolving wheel of content downloads. The rapid pace of today's digital business landscape rarely affords the luxury of prolonged introspection. Overanalysis is like glorified guesswork and is often the norm at large companies. But how do you strike the balance to make sure you've covered the important bits? By trusting your intuition and expertise cultivated over time. By recognizing that every decision won't be flawless, but inaction is a flaw in itself. If you overanalyze, you merely postpone receiving immensely valuable real-world feedback about your ideas, which you can use to inform future decisions. Act first and assess later.

Mitch

ZEN + NETWORKING = MORE PROSPERITY

In 2010, New York was my classroom and the city's top advertising agencies—Deutsch, Ogilvy, Droga5, Wunderman, and more—were my teachers. Here I was, in large glass-fronted meeting rooms, listening to pitches from the crème de la crème of the advertising industry: ultra creatives, charming deviants, and quirky storytellers. But amongst this crowd of ad maestros, there was Gregg, owner of a $50+ million ad agency and the eventual winner of our pitch. What set him apart wasn't just his skill—it was his demeanor: sincere and humble, a stark contrast to his peers. Curiosity got the better of me and I asked Gregg, "What's your secret? How did you build a $50 million ad agency?" His reply was as unexpected as it was simple: "Zen."

Zen:

"Relaxed and not worrying about things that you cannot change."

—Cambridge Dictionary

Zen, he explained, wasn't just a buzzword; it was about being fully present. To Gregg, "Zen" was more than a philosophical concept; it was a practical business strategy. When you're in the moment, you're more in tune with your clients' needs, the market's pulse, and those subtle opportunities that slip by unnoticed. It's about letting go of what you can't control—your image, your perceptions of others, and your predefined business expectations.

While it's essential to be passionate about your projects, non-attachment means not getting overly entangled in the outcomes. This freedom allows you to make clearer decisions, connect easier with others and prevents emotional burnout. Startups, Gregg imparted, aren't just about transactions; they're about genuine connections—essentially, the quality of your network.

When starting out, networking stands out as a cardinal pillar in your toolkit. Often, the depth and breadth of our connections define your growth trajectory. Yet, the art of networking isn't merely about LinkedIn connections or X's followers. Gregg's Zen approach taught me the essence of being truly present in the moment. When applied to networking, this means genuinely listening, authentically engaging, and opening oneself to the endless possibilities each interaction offers. In the realm of

Zen, every encounter is an exchange of energies, an opportunity to discover and be discovered.

I've lived and thrived in 8 different countries. Each move was a fresh start: building wealth, forming friendships, finding my rhythm. And in each place, it was the genuine connections that made the difference. They cleared my vision, allowing me to see opportunities where others saw none. Zen isn't just philosophy; it's a powerful tool for entrepreneurs. It worked for Gregg, it worked for me, and it can work for you too. Remember, every encounter is an opportunity in disguise: your next blockbuster product, maybe a money making partnership, or just finding a like minded genius. So next time you network, really listen. Be there. Who knows what opportunities you'll discover.

EINSTEIN WITHOUT A BRAIN

I've run multiple businesses since 2010, juggling multiple tasks and launching products simultaneously with zero staff, inhouse teams, or outsourced contractors. I couldn't have done it without having a clear personal strategy. Whether you're thinking of taking your solo business to the next level or starting a new project, the level of success will be determined by your strategy. Having a clear personal strategy or blueprint has helped me plan, organize, and steer my projects past $900K+ in revenue. Without a clear blueprint you'll fall in either of two camps:

A: You don't start

B: You start but you float with little progress

"Strategy" can be simplified as follows:

Strategy = I think

Tactics = I do

More specifically:

Strategy = Ambitions, Ideation, Analysis, Planning

Tactics = Mechanisms, Activities, Tasks

And if you drill down even more:

Strategy – Tactics = Einstein's brain in a jar

Tactics – Strategy = Einstein without a brain

Strategy + Tactics = Growth

Before you dive headfirst into building your empire, it's crucial to nail down your personal strategy. Your personal strategy will serve as an actionable blueprint, delineating your ambitions, competencies, and the requisite tactics to start building your powerhouse, i.e., your business. Think of it as your roadmap—it's going to guide every step you take towards success. Without this game plan, you're like a ship without a rudder, floating aimlessly in the sea of business. A lack of a defined personal strategy can lead to a diminished focus and motivation, essential for achieving your objectives and devising forward-moving tactics. It could also lead to potential customer disorientation, unfocused product offerings, and a vague purpose of your solo enterprise. Remember your personal strategy will guide your business strategy. The skeleton of your personal strategy will look like this:

THE PERSONAL STRATEGY

Strategy

Personal:
- What are my true passions & obsessions?
- What am I good at?
- What makes me unique?
- What type of lifestyle do I want to have?
- How do I develop what I love?

Business:
- How do I turn my unique passions & experience into products or services?
- Who's my ideal customer?
- How do I market my products or services?

Tactics

- Pay attention to what you're drawn to
- Make a list of activities that energize you
- Ask close friends & family what they think your passions are
- Review and reflect on your past successes and achievements
- Join clubs or online groups related to your passion

- Identify gaps in the market by prompting AI chatbots
- Talk to potential customers
- Analyze current customer data if available
- Choose appropriate marketing channels
- Create a content calendar

Tools + Apps + Checklists

Strategy + Tactics = Growth

A solid personal strategy will help you answer some big questions right from the start:

1. What's your superpower? What gets you out of bed in the morning? Or put differently, what are your core competencies and driving passions?

2. How can you nurture and grow your passions into something more? Or how can you cultivate and expand upon what you're passionate about?

3. Can you really make money from scratch, without prior experience? Is it possible to generate revenue with little or no experience?

4. Got big dreams but a small wallet? How do you kickstart your business without any funds?

5. Decisions, decisions! Content creation, e-commerce, retail, finance—what's your focus going to be? What's my business really?

6. To team up or not to team up? That's a question to ponder. Is a collaborative approach with a partner more advantageous, or should I proceed independently?

7. What's your secret sauce? What services or products will you bring to the table? What unique value proposition will my services or products provide?

8. Niche market or broad audience—which target suits your arrow? Should I specialize in a niche market or cater to a broader audience?

9. New customers don't grow on trees, so where and how do you find them? What are the most effective strategies and channels for attracting new customers?

10. Is content really king for attracting new customers, or are there alternative strategies to consider?

Bonus:

To grow your business, you'll likely face three challenges: 1) growing an audience, 2) finding time for everything and 3) knowing how to make money.

We've designed Growthapp.co to address these three challenges. It has features, content and tools to rapidly scale your ideas into a money generating machine. Sign up here www.growthapp.co and be one of the first 100 entrepreneurs to get lifetime free access.

AVOID THE TURQUOISE SEA OF SAMENESS

Can your personal strategy really drive a successful startup? In order to answer this question, we'd need to answer another question first: Does your strategy harness your true edge? Let's explore.

Navigating the world of business can sometimes feel like being in a tennis match. Think about Roger Federer, one of the greatest tennis legends, the maestro from Switzerland. Over the past ten years, he's been making headlines, and for good reason. Seventeen Grand Slam titles and reaching Wimbledon finals nine times? The guy's been on fire! Over a decade, he's crafted a legacy that's hard to beat.

But have you ever wondered why Federer pockets so much cash? Sure, he's an exceptional player. But there's more to the story. Think about it. If Federer played badminton, even if he was the best, he wouldn't be raking in as much. Why's that? Federer's tennis skills? That's a "skills" (proprietary) advantage. But tennis being more lucrative than other sports?

Yes. That's a "market" (positional) advantage. Big difference.

"Proprietary Advantage vs Positional Advantage"

Put differently, if Federer chose a different sport, say ping pong, he'd still be awesome, but he wouldn't shine so brightly in that sport. Sometimes, it's not just about your skills but also the market you choose. As an entrepreneur, it's crucial to recognize your "skills" advantage—your unique gifts, obsessions, and talents. But equally important is understanding the terrain or market you're in—that's your positional advantage. If you choose the wrong market to play in, your chances of success could be diminished.

Shifting gears to the business world: If you're not crystal clear on what sets you apart, your strategy might end up in the dumps. Your journey might sometimes feel like sipping a $5 coffee and pondering why the farmer, despite all their hard work, only gets pennies while the coffee shop earns substantially more and can upsell muffins and avocado toast. The true value of your offering is often in the rare, the unique, in what only you bring to the table. It's about mastering your genius, finding that sweet spot, and then playing on the right court. It boils down to this: Money flows to where it's scarce. Always ask: What's rare in my business that will give me an edge and set me apart?

In essence, it's about understanding the real reason why those dollars are rolling in. It's like our Federer example: Find what makes you unique and understand the playing field you're on. That's how you'll not just play, but win and inspire.

THE SEX VS CASH METHOD

I've had infinite conversations with company executives, startup founders, and armchair economists about pursuing "niche market" or "mass market." They would ask me, where should we focus our attention and time? Should we take on more consulting projects or focus on our products or sell more coaching sessions? Their story evolved like this: "Our product or service appeals to a broad audience. I don't want to specialize because I may miss out on other opportunities!" When you're first starting out on your journey, it's hard to choose between Specialist vs Generalist or Niche or Mass Market. Enter the "Sex vs Cash Method" by Hugh MacLeod.

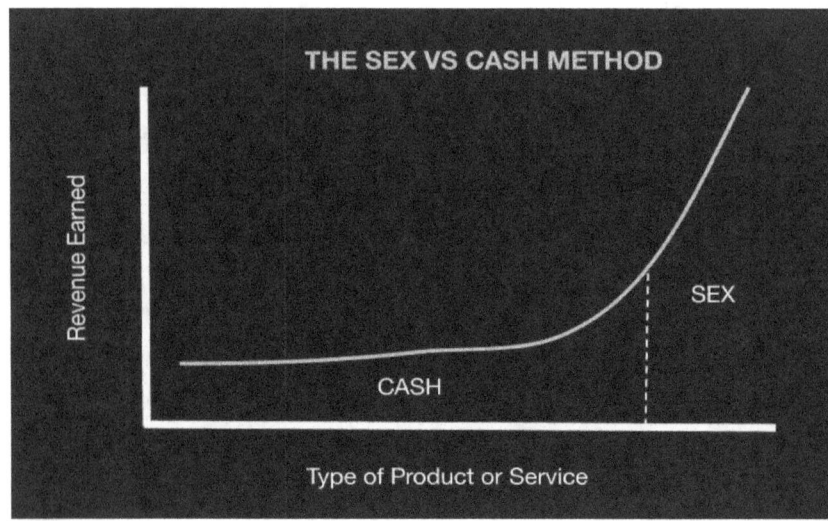

If you're diving into the solopreneur world, you'll feel this method deep in your bones. Picture this: You've got two types of projects in your life. The first one is all glitter and rainbows; we're talking about the stuff you love, the stuff you'd do even if you weren't getting paid—that's the Sex stuff. The second type is the bread and butter—the gigs you take to make sure you're not living in a van under a bridge. That's your Cash work. Or to put it another way: You are both the dreamer and the executor. On one hand, you're given the divine gift of projects that light up your soul— these are your sunrises, your first kisses, your 'aha!' moments that keep you fueled in your solo quest. This is the "Sex," the irreplaceable joy that makes life worth living. Yet, standing equally tall is the sobering reality of your needs—the rent, the groceries, the silent ticking of the clock reminding you that life, as beautiful as it is, also calls for stability. This is your "Cash," the anchor that keeps your ship safe in the harbor, allowing you to venture out to uncharted waters with a return ticket.

Now, you might be thinking, "I'm running my own solo gig; shouldn't I be doing what I love all the time? Shouldn't I be embracing my obsessions?" Well, sure, that's the dream, but let's be honest. Even when you're your own boss, you're going to end up doing work that's all about keeping the lights on. You'll be juggling between client work that doesn't excite you but pays well, and passion projects that might just pay off hugely in the long run. That's ok; it's part of the game.

For solopreneurs, this method is a sanity-saver. How? Well, knowing that it's totally normal to balance between these two types of work helps you keep things in perspective. You can diversify your portfolio to include both the Sex and Cash categories. For example, you might do client consulting work that's not super exciting, but it funds your real passion— maybe creating your own digital courses or writing that book you've been dreaming of.

And here's the amazing thing: Sometimes, you find a project that's a double whammy. It's thrilling and pays well. When that happens, celebrate like you've won the lottery, because, my friend, those gigs are like unicorns.

So, go ahead, use this method to guide your business decisions. Sprinkle in some sexy, creative projects that make your soul dance while also tackling the nitty-gritty stuff that guarantees you'll eat something other than boiled ramen this month. It's not a contradiction; it's the balanced life of a savvy entrepreneur!

THE PHILOSOPHY OF PLUMBING

Everyone's telling you the same old recipe for growing your business online. Share your story, write some blogs or posts, throw in a freebie to get emails, and bang, make money! It's the age-old playbook for content creators' success. But not every game is won with the same moves.

The recipe usually looks like this:

1. **Write your story.** Share your unique experiences, passions and the challenges you have overcome.

2. **Turn your story into content.** Write articles, blog posts, or books about your story. Create videos, podcasts, or social media posts that share your insights.

3. **Create a lead magnet.** Offer something of value to your audience in exchange for their contact information. This could be a short guide, a checklist, or a free consultation.

4. **Monetize your audience.** Once you have built a following, you can start to monetize your audience. This could involve selling digital

products or services, offering coaching or consulting, or creating affiliate links.

But let's pause and think about my buddy Jan, the no-nonsense Dutch plumber. Jan's got years under his belt and a straight-shooting attitude. Do you think he needs to spend years blogging to fix someone's leaky faucet? People aren't going to read 20 articles on why Jan's the "Plumber Guru" before they call him. They've got a problem, and they need it solved, like, yesterday. When you have a flooded kitchen, you're not prompting ChatGPT or Googling articles—you're looking for someone who can fix it, and fix it now. Jan wins trust in that moment because he understands what his customer really wants: a quick, reliable solution. Jan's got other ways to show he's the real deal. Maybe it's stellar branding or a bunch of raving reviews. So, before you dive headfirst into the "content is king" pool, stop and think. Your startup or business might need a totally different playbook. Don't just hope your strategy works; make sure it fits what you're actually trying to do.

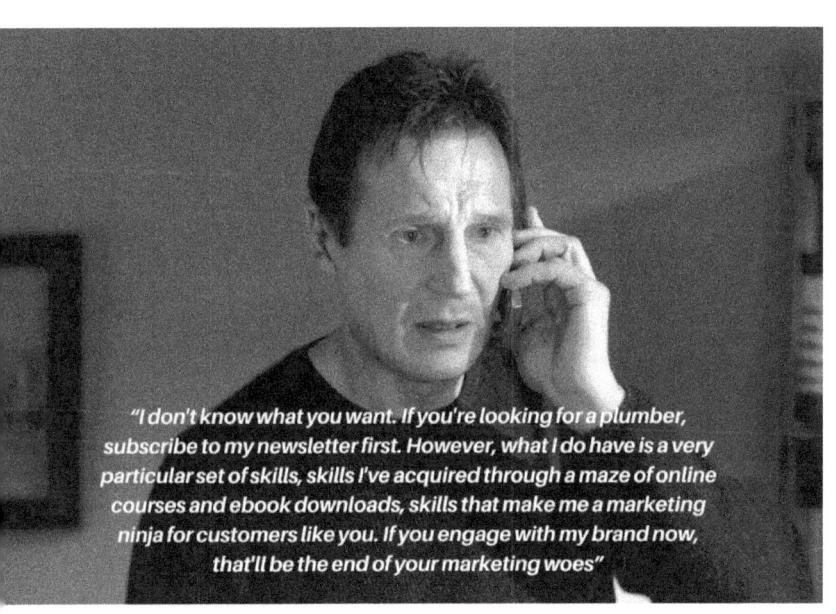

"I don't know what you want. If you're looking for a plumber, subscribe to my newsletter first. However, what I do have is a very particular set of skills, skills I've acquired through a maze of online courses and ebook downloads, skills that make me a marketing ninja for customers like you. If you engage with my brand now, that'll be the end of your marketing woes"

You don't have to follow the online gurus' advice to be a leader in your field. The key isn't to copy the guru's sole marketing tactic but to choose the ones that resonate with your business and your customers. Maybe your gold isn't in blog posts, YouTube videos or podcasts, or even email marketing. Maybe it's just in a killer branding strategy, a bucketload of customer testimonials, or simply being the local go-to person in your area.

THE PHILOSOPHY OF PEDRO THE MAVERICK

Meet Pedro, the Maverick. Unlike Jan, the plumber, Pedro recognizes the current evolving landscape of business and trends. He knows that markets are changing and knows there are new bigger opportunities for scaling his business. Where is he based? Doesn't really matter as much as it used to. What's important now? Adapting to shifting hyper consumer behaviors and leveraging AI tech advancements. Pedro epitomizes the modern solopreneur—ambitious and strategically contrarian.

Pedro's clued in. He knows that just solving prospects' problems is not enough, you've got to give humans hope, a glimpse of a better future. It's about envisioning and articulating a brighter future for his audience. So many businesses hammer on about the nitty-gritty, logical benefits of what their products have to offer. But for startups – especially those targeting the digitally-native hyper consumer segment market – your ongoing marketing communications is about two things specifically: brand awareness (hope) and efficient lead

"Mavericks are visionaries who want to achieve what's never been achieved before. They're not fans of the status quo and will shake things up. Mavericks tend to be innovative, influential, daring, and direct—with a remarkably high tolerance for taking chances. They believe there is a bigger, better, stronger, faster way."

generation. Awareness builds trust with your customers and points to a better, more prosperous future, while lead generation is about the mechanisms and tactics to drive a constant influx of potential customers. Balancing these two elements not only ensures sustained brand visibility but also drives consistent revenue streams.

Then comes the big moment. You've painted a future so bright your customers have to wear shades and you have convinced them you have the tools to solve their problems. Now, here's some science stuff; to guarantee a purchase you have to hit your customers' "Hedonic Hotspots." Imagine a magic button in the brain—when pressed, it goes, "Wow, this feels amazing!" That's the hotspot. It's that Eureka moment when your customer thinks, "Pedro, you're the best!" This real neurological trigger, when activated, resonates profoundly with consumers, reinforcing brand loyalty. It's the point in time where your customer acknowledges the unparalleled value of your offering. On the flip side, miss their hotspots, and they're out the door. If you want to be that entrepreneur who makes the cash register sing and tickles their hedonic hotspots, you need three things: 1) unwavering trust, 2) unequivocal value proposition, and 3) an amazing user experience (UX). These elements collectively influence a consumer's purchasing decision. You need all three to make them happily part with their hard-earned cash. Think back to when you got that Christmas gift you'd been dreaming of. Pure joy, right? It was perfect, it felt right, and unwrapping it? Best. Feeling. Ever.

Here's the deal:

- A blend of trust and value, without superior UX, results in customer dissatisfaction.

- Deliver on value and user experience, but fall short on trust? They might buy, but they'll hesitate.

- Exceptional user experience and trust, but lacking in value? You're shouting into the void.

Simple as that.

The Hedonic Hotspot:

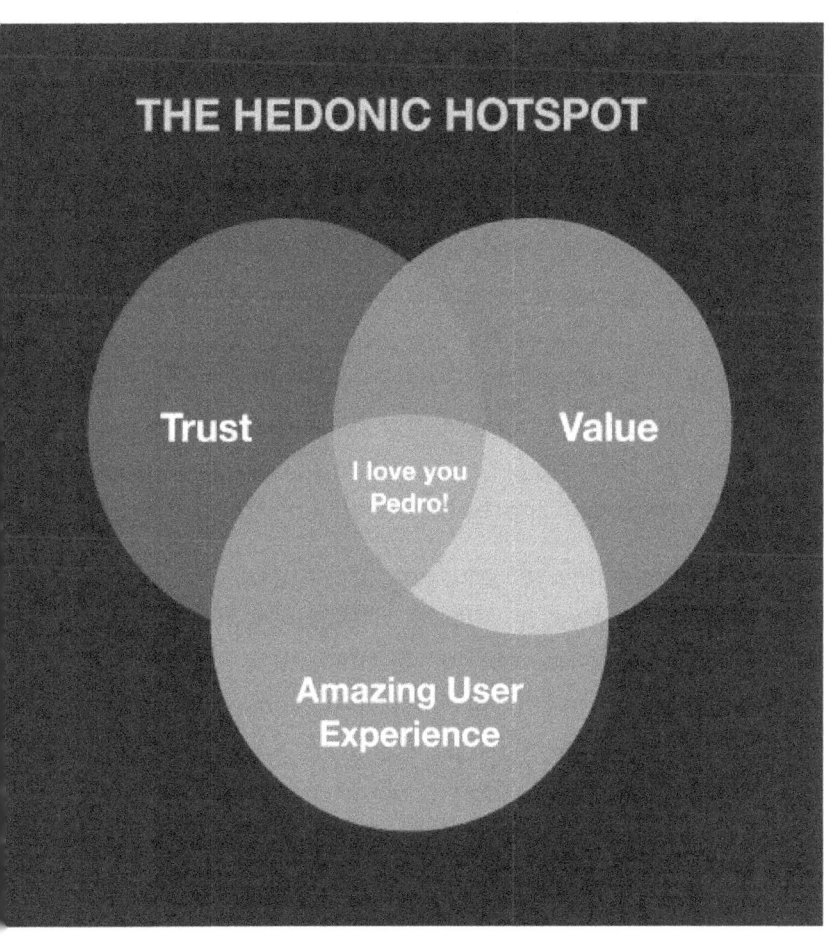

REVENUE IS GENERATED IN THE NEXUS

Understanding the concept of the "business nexus" is essential for strategic revenue generation. A "nexus" isn't just a dictionary term meaning connection or linkage; it's a systematic approach to cultivating customer relationships and driving sales. Particularly for digital product or creator businesses, the success of your revenue generation efforts is determined by the systematic approach of product introductions.

So, here's the deal: your product or service? It's great. But on its own, it isn't the sole money maker. What really brings in revenue is the entire journey you create around your products and services. Think of it like the different stages you walk a friend through when introducing them to your favorite Netflix show. It's all about timing and sequence.

I have used this approach successfully since 2009. Let's break it down:

1. The Teaser: This is the free stuff you put out there, your initial content and first touchpoint. Maybe it's those Instagram posts, blog articles, LinkedIn posts, or that handy little tool you designed. It's what gets people to stop and say, "Hey, who's this?" It's your professional handshake, offering value and introducing your brand to potential customers.

2. The Intro: Imagine giving your friend a trailer or sneak peek of that show. That's your low-cost or free product. This stage involves a low-barrier offer, allowing prospects to further familiarize themselves with your brand. It could be a sample chapter, a mini-course, or a webinar. You're giving them just enough to make them hungry for more.

3. The Main Event: Here's where the magic happens. This is your main product, your flagship. The one that solves problems and gets rave reviews. This is like the first season they binge-watch all night! This is the cornerstone of your business—the primary offering that addresses the specific needs of your clientele. Ensuring excellence and value here is paramount, as this represents the primary source of your revenue.

4. The Bonus Rounds: These are your add-ons. Think of them as the spin-off series or behind-the-scenes clips. Maybe it's an advanced course, one-on-one sessions, or a detailed guide that complements your main offer. After establishing trust with your main offering, these are additional products or services you can provide as an upsell or cross-sell.

And you will read this special offer message last

YOU WILL READ THIS TEASER MESSAGE FIRST

And then you will read about our free course

Then you will consider buying our main product

In essence, the business nexus is about methodically guiding your potential customers through a journey—from initial awareness to loyal patronage. For entrepreneurs, mastering this approach ensures not just sporadic sales but sustained revenue growth. The key takeaway? It's not just about what you're selling. It's about the journey you take your audience on, from curious browsers to raving fans. That journey, that connection – that's your nexus. And when done right, it's a game changer. So, how will you set up your nexus to engage and convert?

WHAT IS A CUSTOMER ACQUISITION ENGINE? (AND HOW TO CREATE ONE)

In the previous story, I introduced the idea of the business nexus, which is an approach for gradually presenting your products and services to your potential buyers. The nexus is particularly important for solopreneurs, digital product or creator businesses, because it allows you to introduce your knowledge and products in an organized fashion to the market. The nexus is your product mix, the type and number of products or services in your company. The Customer Acquisition Engine (CAE) on the other hand, is the process and steps for implementing your Nexus. Think of the Customer Acquisition Engine as a funnel, the set of tasks, flows, and technology for automating your Nexus.

Nexus and Customer Acquisition Engine:

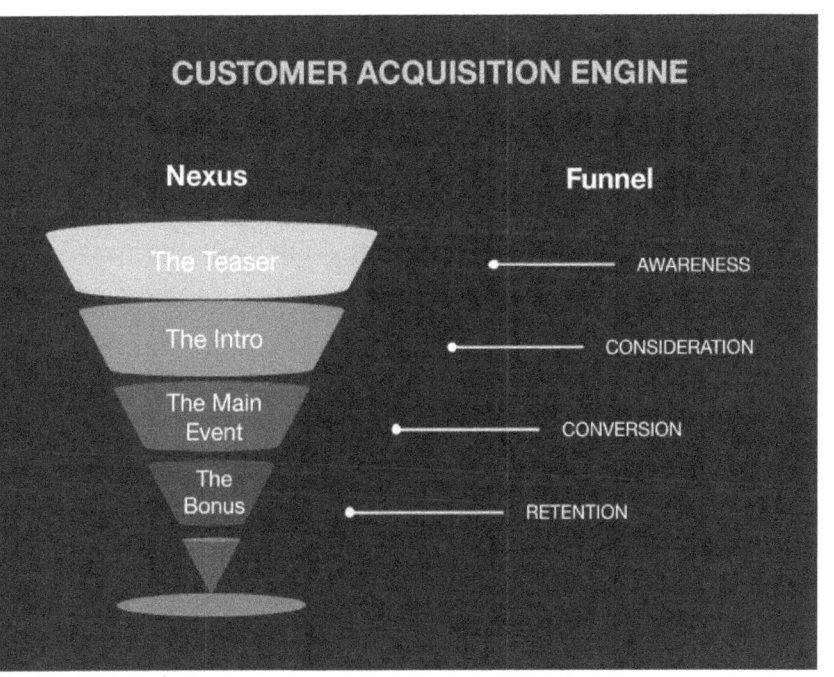

I'll be using the words Engine and Funnel interchangeably as they mean the same thing. Creating customer acquisition funnels doesn't have to be a complex process but it's essential if you want to implement your business nexus and consequently generate revenue.

Imagine a customer acquisition funnel as an army of sales people at your disposal, finding and talking to potential buyers on your behalf. A funnel is a tool that encourages people to engage with your business, moving through several stages to an end point: making a purchase and developing trust in you. Without a well-designed process, some prospects are inevitably going to fall by the wayside. A customer acquisition funnel will help you bring those numbers down, converting more prospects into customers. A funnel, when set up correctly, will attract browsers from across the web, be it social media, Google, paid advertising, and email and convert these browsers into potential customers. Besides presenting products in an orderly sequence, the purpose of the funnel is also to "warm up" or nurture your prospects into getting comfortable with you. Imagine going on a series of dates. First, you bump into each other at a cafe and exchange numbers; the second time, you meet for drinks, then pizza on the third date; and finally something more substantial on the fourth date.

As shown in the illustration above, at each stage of the funnel you'll offer the interested person a specific product, an object of their desire to build trust and authority. Each product of the nexus corresponds to a stage in the funnel. For example, The Teaser product, being a free offer, works great as a way to attract buyers and to generate initial *awareness* of your company. The Intro does wonders in the *consideration* stage as the potential prospect is actively testing and considering your product. Once they've tasted the product and seen the potential results and benefits to their lives, there is a greater likelihood they'll buy or *convert* to The Main Event, which is where you make the bulk of your profits. If you have impressed the buyer with your Main Event product and solved their problem, it will be easier to introduce The Bonus product at a future date. The Bonus product is an additional offer related to the Main Even product, i.e., more revenue—the cherry on top. It's the product that *retains* or keeps the customer loyal to your brand.

The order and introduction of the products are important as you'd want to engage people gradually and build up the interest over time. The warm up or nurturing period will depend on your type of business, the product, and the urgency of the problem you're solving for your customer.

There are 3 important things you need to consider when implementing your Customer Acquisition Engine:

1. You must attract a lot of potential buyers in the awareness stage.

    Marketing is both a numbers and a percentage game, especially at the top of the funnel. You have to cast a wide net and appeal to a broad range of potential customers. The higher the volume of people entering into your funnel, the higher the number of potential sales at the other end. And only a percentage of people entering the funnel will respond. Another percentage of those will respond with interest. A percentage of those who are interested will eventually turn into a sale.

2. Don't be boring.

    Unless you run an open heart surgery tool company, your messaging doesn't have to be too safe or corporate. If you're going to get the attention of people and break through the noise online, you're going to have to be ultra creative and write quality content that not only captures their attention but also arouses their imagination. Remember you're competing for their attention against 100's of other creators, Netflix, big brands, news flashes, Instagram, kids, etc. It's an attention economy.

3. Choose simple tech.

    Let's continue with the assumption that you're a one person business or an early startup with 2–4 people. Small teams by their very nature are agile and can make decisions quickly. Your goal at the beginning of your journey should be to use the least possible structure and technology to support and inspire your partners and any freelancers. This is what a typical marketing technology toolkit would look like for a startup:

- ChatGPT or similar to help you write content and posts for your Teaser

- Landing page builder

- List manager or customer relationship manager (CRM) for managing and segmenting your contacts into lists

- Email tool for emailing your contacts and automating the emailing process

- Product page or website with payment processing tool

Table 1: Marketing Technology Toolkit

Generative AI	ChatGPT, Claude, Bard AI
Landing page builder	Leadpages, Carrd, ConvertKit, FlowTrack, Unbounce
List manager or CRM	Pipedrive, Snovio, Zoho CRM, Keap, Outseta
Email tool***	MailerLite, Mailchimp, ActiveCampaign, Constant Contact, Drip, GetResponse
Product page or website	Gumroad, Kajabi, Teachable, WordPress, Squarespace, Webflow

We have tested most of these

*** Illustrative examples; these are good options to consider but do your research*

*** Many email apps have integrated a landing page builder and list managers / CRM*

Special mention: If you're planning on selling digital courses then there are tools in the market that incorporate several apps into one tool (landing page

+ list manager + course builder + email app). For example: ConvertKit, FlowTrack, Gumroad, Kajabi, Teachable, LoopGenius, Clickfunnels, Thinkific.

THE INFLUENCE OF THE UNKNOWN

Absolute control is an illusion. No matter how hard you try to plan and control your startup, there are invisible forces and hidden systems influencing the outcomes. Creativity, planning, applying your knowledge, and sheer determination are for sure part of the business equation and a predictor of success. But these elements are only one part of the equation. Let's not sugarcoat it; building a startup is tough. 90% of them fail and 70% of them don't live to see five years old.

You often hear online about "secret" success formulas that are focused primarily on understanding your processes and that can be copied and applied in your business. The idea is if you know and link your processes from marketing and technology, to delivery in a cohesive flow, you'll then improve your output, increase your speed of operations, and win more customers and revenue.

It's about looking at your business as a series of connected systems, much like cogs in a machine. It's a practical, logical, military command and control type of approach, asking us to view business as interconnected gears in a vast machine—very left-brained, where logic and analysis reside. But this system's approach is based largely on being able to see the interaction between moving parts, and may oversimplify the myriad complexities of business. While this process approach offers an intriguing lens through which to view and organize your startup, let's consider the idea that a business is more profound and richer than just a collection of interconnected systems. Your entrepreneurial journey isn't just a systematic series of steps; it's a dynamic dance between structure and improvisation, planning and spontaneity.

Navigating the uncharted waters of entrepreneurship is more than just tweaking processes and setting goals; it's about embracing the unknown, managing complex human relationships, and letting your creativity fly. Running your business is inherently chaotic and unpredictable, filled with variables that aren't easily quantifiable or understandable. There are elements within your company—sales, market expansion, people, programming, and content creation—that are not easily reducible to a systems model because of the profound unpredictability and the influence of the unknown.

Why is this important? External factors from customer behavior, technology, and market dynamics are in constant flux. Extensive research shows that 80% of what makes companies grow isn't so much about their set up, their value propositions, or their business models. Rather, a startup's growth is fundamentally determined by their selected markets—by the specific domains in which they choose to compete. Take for example the Customer Relationship Management (CRM) software market. It's a growing market but a very saturated one to enter. There's of course always room for innovation and new ideas and you could launch your CRM startup and succeed. But chances are it will be tougher to grow and win. Not only will you start in a competitive space but you'll also need to convince buyers to try your unknown product or switch over to a new tool.

The Marketing Technology Landscape 2023

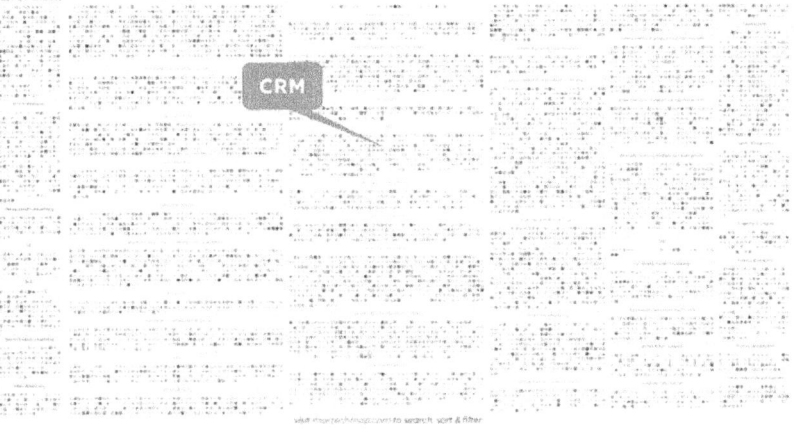

(Each dot represents a company) Souce: chiefmartec.com

Achieving clarity and specificity in identifying your markets is paramount—it facilitates a more profound understanding and enlightened personal strategy. The challenge for strategic minds is to allocate a substantial majority of their efforts—80% or more— in two key activities: 1) clearly defining your customers' problems and 2) finely delineating your markets and making informed decisions about where to allocate your resources and where to compete. This precision and commitment in strategy formulation and resource allocation are the linchpins of achieving entrepreneurial success.

The sharper and clearer you are about your markets, the better you'll understand the underlying trends and the better you'll be able to compete against thousands of other businesses online. Does your strategy pack a secret punch? Do you possess knowledge that remains elusive to your competitors? Relying solely on conventional analysis of data yields only commonplace insights. To truly stand out, you need that golden nugget of insight that others don't have.

Consider the example of the Centers for Disease Control and Prevention (CDC) in the US. One would anticipate that the CDC, with its extensive network of healthcare professionals reporting in real-time, would possess the most timely information regarding any outbreaks. However, in an intriguing twist, it is Google that has surpassed them in this domain. The reason is surprisingly simple: Individuals tend to search for flu-related symptoms on Google as soon as they experience them, providing Google with immediate and precise data on the spread of any disease.

The takeaway is clear: Dig deeper, look beyond the obvious, and find that unique insight that'll give you an edge. You must seek out and leverage those distinct insights that others overlook. It's this depth of understanding that will solidify your strategic positioning and propel your business forward.

WHAT CONTENT DO PEOPLE CRAVE?

If you're looking to truly connect and vibe with your audience, it's all about publishing content they can't resist. There are 10 types of content that people just *love*. These are foundational types of content that have consistently shown to engage users effectively over the years. Think of them as your content toolkit. For instance, everyone adores a story about achieving your dreams—it's just human nature. Here's the golden tip: Use these content types as a lens to frame your content writing and stories. It's like what the legendary ad guru, Leo Burnett, once said: "Make it simple. Make it memorable. Make it inviting to look at and make it fun to read." And don't worry too much about being grammatically perfect. Solid research indicates that about 70% of users prioritize authenticity and relatability over ultra polished, high production quality in social media content.

WHAT CONTENT DO THEY CRAVE?

1| Content that reminds them that life is short

2| Content that reminds us that dreams can come true

3| Content that gives us faith to believe in bigger things

4| Content that reminds us that we matter

7| Content that makes us smile or laugh

5| Content that has unexpected twists

6| Content that tells a captivating story

8| Content that inspires us to action

9| Content that reveals secrets

10| Content that educates us

11| Content that tells that anything is possible

HOW TO WRITE CONTENT THAT SELLS

Too many entrepreneurs get tangled up in the same two problems: 1) How do I persuade someone to buy from me using nothing but the written word and 2) how can someone who isn't a professional writer still write compelling, persuasive, believable content?

Selling is at the heart of your business. Selling is not about talking or manipulating someone into buying your products or services. Selling involves active listening, asking the right questions, psychology, and timing. It's about communicating genuinely and adding value to the buyers' life. It's about solving a specific problem at a price the buyer is willing to pay.

"Pretend that every single person you meet has a sign around his or her neck that says, 'Make me feel important.' Not only will you succeed in sales, you will succeed in life." —Mary Kay Ash

During 2010–2017, I founded and ran a successful 13+ people digital marketing agency before selling it and merging it with Deloitte. I can say with 100% certainty that selling was one of or the most important factor in the success of my company. Everything we did was about communicating. Every email, proposal, PowerPoint, and content piece was deliberately written to sell and influence. Every opportunity to connect online or in person was focused on one thing—persuasion. To get our message across we told one consistent story for 7 years straight. We did not deviate. This was the message:

Many have the wrong perception about selling, thinking that selling is too "salesly." Many startup founders delegate sales and marketing activities to managers hoping to avoid selling and rejection. I'd like to present a different way to think about selling and writing, shift your perspective so you'll see the huge advantages of adopting a natural communication style.

WHY YOU MUST FOCUS ON THE BUYER

There are two simple reasons why you have to write for your buyer— not your boss, not your investor, not your colleagues, or yourself. And it has to do with the attention and the level of investment they make in your writing. Picture this: Your reader cozied up at home or maybe scanning through Instagram during a quick office break. They've received a nostalgic WhatsApp from an old friend from Paris, an email of their favorite podcast with a freebie attached, and then there's your email, tweet, or LinkedIn post.

Your piece is the wild card here. It's the one thing they didn't ask for, pay for, or have any emotional connection to. Even though they fall in your "demographics," they don't know who you are.

When people feel invested in something, and it pulls at either their heartstrings or their wallet, they'll read it. Even if it's peppered with spelling errors and faulty grammar, they'll power through because they care. But without that connection? They're not giving it a pass.

So what's the secret sauce? Write a message that's undeniably for them. Put yourself in their shoes and dive into their world, their lives, their worries, their day-to-day. Make it sound like they're part of a tribe. And wrap it up with such smooth, effortless English that all they see is the message, not the words carrying it. It's a message delivered in such effortlessly good English that they don't notice the writing, just the content.

Effective copy isn't about self-promotion but about providing clear, tangible benefits that resonate with your target audience. "Focusing on The Buyer" is about the need for copywriting to be direct, benefit-driven, and focused on solving your customer's problem or fulfilling their desire. This tactic underscores that many fail by being overly technical, jargon-filled, or company-centric, thereby neglecting to communicate in a manner that is accessible and compelling to the customer.

Pay attention to the following:

Write for Your Customer: Effective copy prioritizes the customer's needs, desires, and problems, writing messages that directly speak to them. Engage your audience by focusing on 'them' rather than using 'we' and 'our,' which tend to be company-focused.

Focus on Strong Headlines: The first thing a potential customer sees is your email subject line, landing page message, or LinkedIn header image. The headline is the "ad of the ad" and what will capture the user's attention. Spend time perfecting the headline.

Avoid Jargon: Accessibility in language is crucial, avoiding technical jargon in favor of clear, simple English language.

Message + Benefits = Hope: The emphasis must be placed on the tangible benefits the customer will derive, rather than mere features of the product or service.

Clarity and Directness: While your content writing can be witty and creative, clarity is more important than just creativity. The primary goal of copy is to sell, not to entertain or show off the writer's cleverness.

The Ultimate Authority: Write content that emotionally resonates with the audience by demonstrating your expertise in a subject matter using your experience, personal story and credible sources for research.

How to apply this in your business:

As a solopreneur, ensure your copy speaks directly to your customer's needs and desires, utilizing a clear, jargon-free language that emphasizes benefits, with a direct call to action, ensuring every word is meticulously chosen to resonate and build a bridge from the customer's problem to your solution.

Bonus:

To grow your business, you'll likely face three challenges: 1) growing an audience, 2) finding time for everything and 3) knowing how to make money.

We've designed Growthapp.co to address these three challenges. It has features, content and tools to rapidly scale your ideas into a money generating machine. Sign up here www.growthapp.co and be one of the first 100 entrepreneurs to get lifetime free access.

ADORE THE IMPERFECT SINNER

Let's dive into the nitty-gritty of human flaws and how they can surprisingly be our secret weapon in writing incredible content. Peel off all our formalities and masks and, what are we? Beautifully imperfect humans. And guess what, all of us have indulged in the seven cardinal sins at some point in our lives. Let's consider the seven sins and how we might use them in our content writing.

"Adore The Sinner, Love The Content"

PRIDE: Everyone loves a little ego boost. Tell your potential buyers how important they are. Shower them with genuine compliments, and tell them you see their hard work and brilliance. Suggest subtly that they're smart decision-makers and then suggest that someone with their obvious talent for making right decisions really should be subscribing, buying or going along with your suggestion.

ENVY: The brilliant Fear of Missing Out or FOMO. Highlight stories of others totally crushing it with your product or service. Showcase how others are already reveling in the awesomeness of what you're selling, creating a buzz they'd want to be part of.

GLUTTONY: Think about it. Who doesn't love that extra scoop of ice cream? If your product or service brings joy, comfort, or even a dash of indulgence, emphasize it. If what you offer brings deep satisfaction to their everyday life, bingo, you've nailed a perfect selling point.

LUST: If you can hint that your offerings will quench some of their deepest desires, then you have hit a gold mine. Think of insatiable lust as a hunger for anything—power, influence, social status, even more dopamine.

ANGER: We've all been there, raging against bad service or a lousy product. Be the hero and offer them an alternative that'll whisk them away from that frustration. If your product solves a major frustration many face, emphasize the solution.

GREED: It's not always about wanting more things or money, but maybe more time, more freedom, more peace of mind. Paint a picture of abundance and make them see the bigger pie. It's a magnet they can't resist.

SLOTH: Laziness is our cozy friend. Showcase how your product is the comfy couch that makes their life effortlessly smooth. Show them how they can accomplish more with less effort.

While people may later justify purchases logically, they buy based on emotion first. So, add a bit of these 'sins' in your content. But, pro-tip: always be smooth and subtle with it. No one likes feeling like they're being played.

3 STEPS TO GETTING YOUR STARTUP ORGANIZED

Have you ever felt swamped by those super complex digital tools? From project management apps, messaging tools, to note takers, they're stuffed with features we never use. Such tools, designed with the requirements of large corporations in mind, impose an unnecessary burden of complexity on small businesses and individual entrepreneurs.

When operating as a sole proprietor or leading a small team, agility and speed are paramount. Simplicity in tools and processes not only enhances efficiency but also paves the way for scalability. This is crucial as we aim for significant business milestones, such as reaching the $1 million revenue mark.

Simplicity isn't just about ease—it's about liberation. It clears the decks so you can zero in on what truly matters: nailing those sales, creating killer content, writing clean code, and dazzling your customers. Fewer features translate to smoother sailing. Quicker decisions, less wrangling, and heaps more room for creativity fosters an environment conducive to innovation.

And let's not forget the elephant in the room; traditional task and project management tools can eat up your time. You find yourself in an endless loop, searching and prompting ChatGPT just to find the stuff you need to get the job done. As founders, it is imperative that we select tools that align with our business needs—tools that are efficient, easy to use, and supportive of our growth trajectory. Simplification is not just an operational choice, but a strategic imperative for the entrepreneur seeking to maximize business potential.

Magical Number 3

As an early startup founder you initially only need three tools:

1. A MVP: Minimum Viable Planner (think Growthapp.co, Remember The Milk or Asana)

2. Google Drive

3. An AI chatbot: ChatGPT, Bard, Jasper, or Claude

THE FLOW ORCHESTRATOR & THE PRODUCT MAESTRO, THE TWO-PERSON $1MILLION BUSINESS OF THE FUTURE

Consider the following:

"Inc. magazine reported that more than **75%** of the *Inc.* 500 companies in 2018 were founded by just one or two people."

All of the companies I founded were started and run by two people. Jivelo, Expandeer, and Maverick Soul. The ideal startup team is often portrayed by VCs, incubators, and academics as a combination of many talented individuals with complementary skills across

"Forbes found that the median team size for unicorn startups was only 2 people."

a range of disciplines. Venture capitalist (VC) firms in particular, and startup incubators, tend to favor teams over sole founders. But put yourself in the VC's shoes; their goal is to sell your startup at a future date at a huge multiple. They're gambling that your startup will be one to their fortune exits so they want assurances your startup is staffed with a team of PhDs (Poor, Hungry & Deft). Nothing wrong with that; they invest and therefore deserve a return on their money. VCs have a vested interest in encouraging larger teams as a requirement for a successful exit. However, VC's opinions and funding are just one of the many options available that you should consider for starting and scaling your business. Don't let the idea of going it alone or in a small team deter you from turning your business idea into reality. With the right strategies and resources, you can absolutely launch and bootstrap a startup on your own. Going solo doesn't necessarily mean doing it all by yourself. When I ran Expandeer, my 13+ person digital marketing agency in 2015, this is what the team structure looked like:

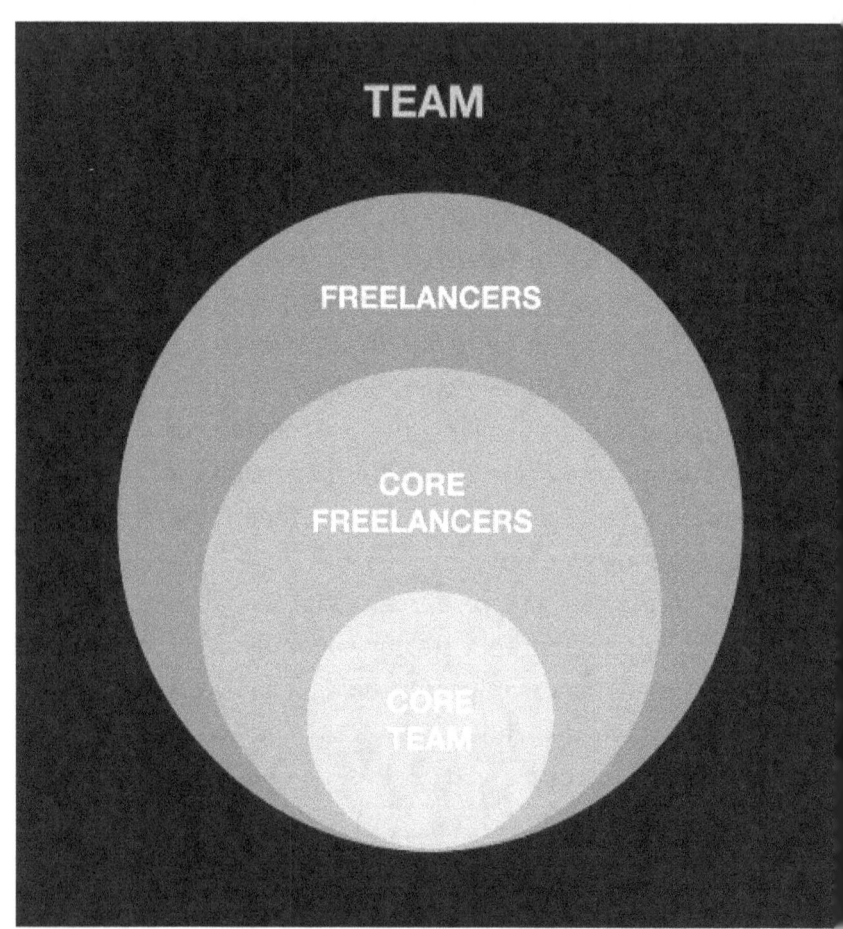

Core Team:

We were two co-founders, each with specific roles in the agency: the Flow Orchestrator and the Product Maestro, each with distinct but sometimes overlapping responsibilities and focus areas.

The Flow Orchestrator (FO) was the hustler and strategist, the person focused on growing the flow of ideas, clients, and revenue. The FO was the creative generalist juggling multiple roles, responsible for marketing, and evangelizing the story, setting the go-to-market strategy and growing sales. He was the savage, the cockroach that wouldn't die, the one with laser focus energy and positivism.

The Product Maestro (PM) was the all around project virtuoso, the one responsible for all product, content, and software delivery activities. The agency wouldn't function without the PM. If the Flow Orchestrator was all about money and goal setting, the Product Maestro was the glue that held the business together and ensured the client was not just happy but ecstatic with the results. Her internal communication and planning skills were world-class.

Core Freelancers:

These were full-time contractors. Their work and deliverables were core to our startup operations and revenue generation. Our goal was to hire the best talent at the best prices regardless of country location. For example, our creative director was based out of Buenos Aires, Argentina. Our paid search specialist worked remotely from Serbia. Two key account directors worked from the beach in Aruba. The SEO expert was located in India and our key developers were based in the US.

Freelancers:

These were part-time contractors. Their work was important but not critical for the delivery of client work or bringing in revenue. For example, all admin work from accounting and tax, human resources, payroll, and legal. All of these can be fully outsourced at the start of your journey. Due to legal requirements or local knowledge, for example, tax and accounting rules, it may be better that these contractors are located in your country of business.

We had the team structure above 8 years ago. A lot has changed since then. Fast forward to 2024. What's different now? Today I'd be able to run the same business with just 2 full-time people and still turn over $1million in revenue. This is what the new structure would look like:

Core team:

- Flow Orchestrator
- Product Maestro

AI and freelancers:

- Creative work

- Accounts / Community management

- AI Agents (SEO, Advertising, Data, more)

- Developers

- Admin (accounting and tax, human resources, payroll to legal)

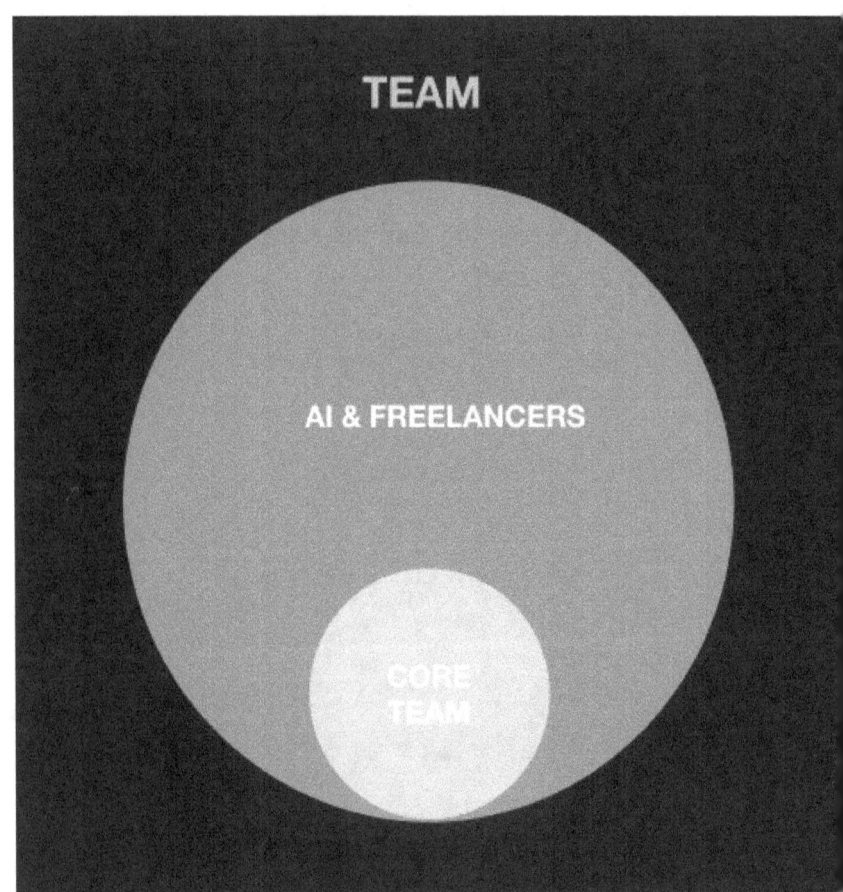

The structure of your team will depend on your specific type of business. If you're a software house then likely the FO or PM would also be the tech lead, writing code for the company or clients. If you're a digital creator or education business, your Product Maestro may likely be the main content strategist.

If you're going to work with remote teams, the following three factors are critical for managing deliverables and accountability successfully.

a. Clear expectations: Set crystal clear rules of engagement for your remote teams. Always be flexible, but establish ground rules that everyone should follow. Since your staff may be in different timezones, don't leave anything to chance.

b. Clear communications: Decide which communication channels you'll use in different situations. For example, you might update freelancers about tasks through a to-do app and use, for example, Slack channels for non-urgent chatting. Also nailing the perfect amount of communication is difficult, so it's better to over communicate rather than under-communicate.

c. Easy task tool: You'll need to invest in a to-do tool to empower your remote teams. Ideally an all-in-one project management or task app with chatting functionality. Alternatively, Slack will also work for small teams.

THE ALGORITHM WILL WIN

Contrary to popular opinion, AI will replace humans. If not now, very soon. We already know that AI and digital can free up valuable time spent on mundane tasks, massively speed up creative work, and automate workflows. AI will not just be a sidekick to enhance your thinking; it will be the central brain within your business. How? As we make progress, more of our thinking will be converted into algorithms. As we progress, more of our execution will be done by algorithms. The real life example below illustrates the power of algorithms vs the human brain. I requested a taxi in two different countries. This is what happened.

Country 1: (Human brain)

Me: Hi, remember me? You dropped us off at the office earlier today. I'd like to order a taxi again. We're ready now. When can we expect the taxi?

Taxi driver: Hmm, I'm actually at the airport now, waiting in line for the next ride. Let me see, I can be there roughly in an hour? (one hour !)

Country 2: (Algorithm)

Me: I get my phone out and tap on DiDi, a taxi ride app (Uber equivalent) and select my location.

Taxi app: Shows the taxi ride details and approximate arrival time of 5 minutes.

Me: I select the taxi ride and the taxi arrives in 3 minutes. I tap on confirm.

"1 Hour vs 3 minutes"

(time it takes a human brain to process information compared to an Algorithm)

When it comes to transactional tasks and even creative types of output, the human brain will not be able to compete against the algorithm. Unless you're a nurse or work at a funeral home, your business, be it a software, creator, education, solo business, ecommerce, finance, etc, will be an algorithm-first business in the future.

25 REASONS WHY LISTS WILL ALWAYS WORK

Here's every unique lesson someone taught me in my 25 year career:

1. It's a world of abundance; there's enough for everyone.

2. Your personal goals will always drive your business goals.

3. Don't take yourself too seriously.

4. Not every idea leads to a pot of gold. You will fail; learn from it.

5. Travel internationally and talk to the locals.

6. Always build people up.

7. Build 2 or 3 superpowers (skills) in your lifetime.

8. Observe the rules, but bend them so they'll work for you.

9. Getting rejected opens doors to new interesting paths.

10. Live spontaneously in the short term, but plan for the long term.

11. No one is coming to save you; it's all in your hands.

12. There's no sign from above; you create your own opportunities.

13. The perfect partner doesn't exist. Focus on their good qualities.

14. Surround yourself with a dreamer, a doer, and a confidant.

15. You must have diabolical laser focus to succeed.

16. It's always day one; there are always new ideas and more opportunities.

17. You're being held back by your unwillingness to take action.

18. You are who you surround yourself with.

19. Everything you need is already within you.

20. It's a circus out there; people will envy you for no reason.

21. Hire for a combination of attitude, curiosity, and results-oriented.

22. A large part of communication is non-verbal.

23. You are what you share.

24. Saying yes to everyone is a losing battle.

25. The best thing a human can do is help another human learn more.

That's it.

Don't take yourself too seriously. (Michael, middle and Guido, right)

CLOSING THOUGHTS

Isn't it wild to think that one simple spark of an idea can ignite the engine of a thriving business? It's like planting a seed in just the right spot, giving it a splash of water and a pinch of soil, and watching it stretch into a magnificent tree. Or imagine this: A single human cell, given the perfect environment, can multiply and blossom into a whole, healthy person. Now, crank that seed image up a notch—with a little space and a timed water system, you've got yourself a forest! It's incredible.

Here's your future: It's 2024, and that same seed magic is happening in the business world. You can catapult a business to the million-dollar mark on the back of a simple idea, mixed in with the right tech, smart processes, and your unstoppable mindset. Gone are the days when business was a playground for big corporations—the ones with large teams, fat budgets, or complex systems. Now, it's all about agility and the everyday heroes—people like you and me, fueled by passion and a vision that can achieve the impossible.

The rise of AI and automation has also redefined the operational blueprint for startups, birthing the concept of "The Two-Person $1 Million Business of The Future: The Flow Orchestrator and the Product Maestro." Businesses are no longer confined to local markets but have the opportunity to tap into global audiences. You will no longer be shackled to a physical location on the map, selling to people who speak only your language. And traditional advertising? Toss it out. Instead, zone in on your "business nexus" to spread your offerings far and wide, consistently.

As we embrace AI and digital, it's crucial to maintain flexibility in our systems and workflows and possess an acute understanding of market trends and customer challenges. It's also time to burn the outdated, safe corporate marketing playbook and, instead, make sure you're hitting your prospects' "hedonic hotspots" – right in the feels, every single time.

Looking ahead to the 2030s, the most successful startups will be those that move beyond the trap of excessive content consumption, the "StuckHome Syndrome," and transition into prolific hyper creators, leveraging AI as a "second brain." The tools and technologies necessary for exponential growth are already at our disposal, ready to be capitalized upon by visionary entrepreneurs. Now it's your turn to step up, carve your path, and watch your business flourish and multiply like never before.

And in those moments of doubt, remember: It's not just possible, it's happening right now.

To your unstoppable growth,

Guido and Michael

--------------END-------------